SPACE CAT EXPLORES **STEM**

All About Systems

by Jacqueline A. Ball
illustrations by Ken Bowser

RED
CHAIR
·PRESS·

Please visit our website at **www.redchairpress.com** for more high-quality products for young readers.

About the Author

Jacqueline A. Ball is a Seattle-based writer, editor, and the former publisher of Scientific American Books for Kids and Weekly Reader Juvenile Book Clubs. Awards and honors include Booklist Top 10 Youth Series Nonfiction (ALA), Children's Choice and Parents' Choice Honors.

Publisher's Cataloging-In-Publication Data
Names: Ball, Jacqueline A. | Bowser, Ken, illustrator.
Title: All about systems / by Jacqueline A. Ball ; illustrations by Ken Bowser.

Description: South Egremont, MA : Red Chair Press, [2017] | Series: Space Cat explores STEM | Interest age level: 006-009. | Aligned to: Next Generation SCIENCE Standards. | Includes glossary, Did You Know sidebars and Try It! feature. | Includes bibliographical references and index. | Summary: "People use creative or inventive thinking to adapt the natural world to help them meet their needs or wants. All people use tools and technology in their life and jobs to solve problems. Join Space Cat on an exploration of systems in both the natural world and in the human-made world. Readers discover how STEM skills keep systems working."--Provided by publisher.

Identifiers: LCCN 2016954285 | ISBN 978-1-63440-195-1 (library hardcover) | ISBN 978-1-63440-199-9 (paperback) | ISBN 978-1-63440-203-3 (ebook)

Subjects: LCSH: System theory--Juvenile literature. | Technology--Juvenile literature. | Systems biology--Juvenile literature. | CYAC: Technology. | Mathematics in nature.

Classification: LCC Q175.3 .B35 2017 (print) | LCC Q175.3 (ebook) | DDC 501--dc23

Photo Credits: Shutterstock, Inc.

Space Cat Explores STEM first published by:
Red Chair Press LLC   PO Box 333   South Egremont, MA 01258-0333

Printed in the United States of America
0517 1P CGBF17

Breathe in. Breathe out.
☑ You're using a **system**.

Turn on a faucet.
☑ You're using a system.

Take a ride on your bike.
☑ You're pedaling a system.

A system is a group of parts that work together to make something happen. Each part of a system has its own job to do. If one part doesn't work right, the whole system will fail. The parts depend on each other, like members of a team.

Large and small systems make the world work. There are systems in the world of nature. There are systems that scientists and engineers invented to make our lives easier, safer, and more fun.

Space Cat and her friend Dog will tell you where to find them, starting with the systems that make *you* work.

Look for important new words in **bold** letters.
Look for systems in red letters. How many did you find?

You breathe thousands of times a day. It happens so often you probably don't even notice. Good thing your lungs are paying attention.

When you breathe in, air travels to your lungs. The air holds oxygen, which all living creatures need to survive. Oxygen mixes with your blood and fills it with **energy**.

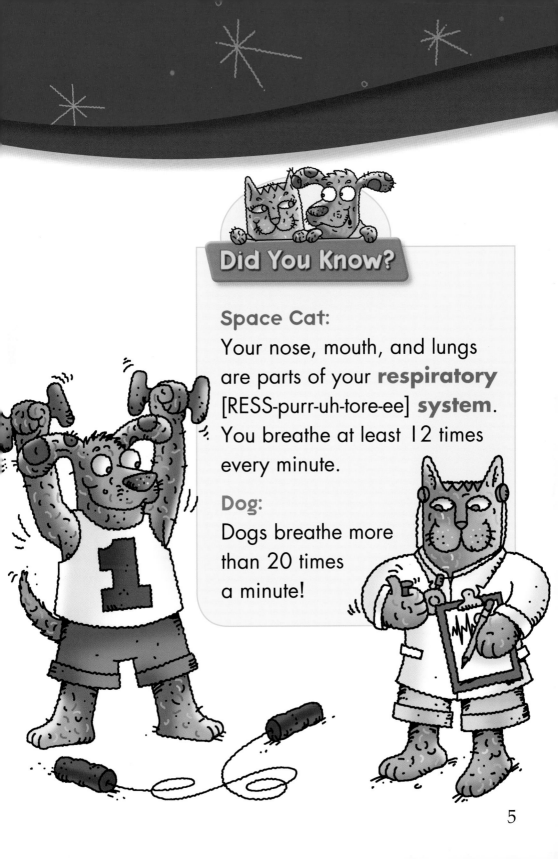

Did You Know?

Space Cat:
Your nose, mouth, and lungs are parts of your **respiratory** [RESS-purr-uh-tore-ee] **system**. You breathe at least 12 times every minute.

Dog:
Dogs breathe more than 20 times a minute!

5

Your heart pumps this powerful blood through tubes called blood vessels. Some tubes are thick. Some are thinner than a thread. Humans have thousands of miles of blood vessels!

After the blood deposits its oxygen throughout your body, it travels back to your lungs. Instead of healthy oxygen, it now carries harmful carbon dioxide. But don't worry. Getting rid of it is easy.

Just breathe out.

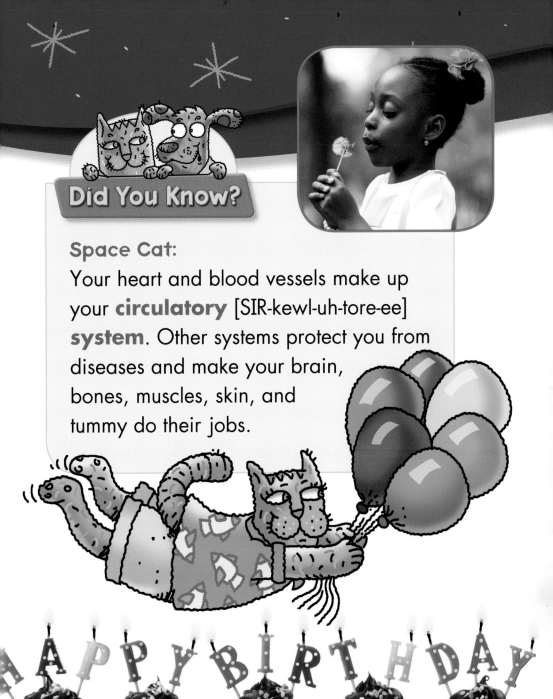

Did You Know?

Space Cat:

Your heart and blood vessels make up your **circulatory** [SIR-kewl-uh-tore-ee] **system**. Other systems protect you from diseases and make your brain, bones, muscles, skin, and tummy do their jobs.

Your circulatory system carries blood where it needs to go in large and small blood vessels. **Transportation systems** carry people where they need to go on highways, streets, tracks, and pathways. Humans invented transportation systems to make travel faster, easier, and safer.

Public transportation systems deliver workers to their jobs on city buses, subways, and light rail. Airplane pilots depend on air traffic control systems to stay in the right flight path and to land safely.

Computers operate most transportation systems and keep them on schedule. If a flight or train is delayed, later ones may be delayed too.

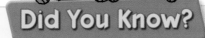

Did You Know?

Space Cat:
Traffic lights **communicate** with drivers. They show when to stop, go, and slow down.

Dog:
My favorite kind of transportation system is walking with my humans.

Communications systems let us share ideas and learn important information. The **Internet** is a modern communication system. The alphabet we use today comes from an **ancient** system that goes back about 4,000 years.

Dialing 911 anywhere in the United States will bring help. It is part of a national emergency communication system.

Hieroglyphics was an ancient form of writing.

EMERGENCY CALL
911

Space Cat:

Write down all the ways living creatures show their thoughts and feelings. Don't forget that not all communication needs words! Work with a friend for more ideas and more fun!

Dog:

Don't forget animals! When I'm happy, I wag my tail.

11

A bicycle is a machine. It's also a system. All of its parts work together so you can take a ride.

Seat

Brakes

Frame

Handlebars

Pedals

Wheels

The frame holds everything together.
The handlebars let you hold on and steer.
The wheels make the bike roll.
The seat gives you a place to sit.
The pedals turn the wheels.
The brakes stop the bike.
What more do you need? Energy! The power to pedal comes from you.

Try it!

Space Cat:

Could you ride a bike with one part missing? Make some bike sketches with different parts removed.

13

After a bike ride, a cold drink of water tastes good. **Plumbing systems** carry water through pipes to faucets and drinking fountains. Other pipes drain used water away when we flush a toilet. One broken or leaky pipe can shut down a plumbing system.

Humans can't survive without water. Our bodies have built-in plumbing systems that use water to fight off illness, digest our food, and get rid of waste.

Did You Know?

Space Cat:

Water makes up more than half your body weight. Drink lots of water every day.

Dog:

Dogs need extra water when the weather is hot. You do too!

A thermostat can control the temperature in a room.

Engineers design **heating systems** to keep buildings warm and comfortable. There are different kinds of heating systems, but many use a furnace that runs on gas or oil. The furnace boils water to heat air. Then a pump forces the air through openings in floors or walls to warm up the rooms.

Most heating and **cooling systems** in buildings are controlled by a **thermostat**. In humans, a special part of the brain acts as a natural thermostat. If you get too cold, it sends a signal to shiver. That produces heat. If you get too hot, it sends a signal to sweat. That cools you down.

Did You Know?

Space Cat:
Humans and other **mammals** are warm-blooded. Our body temperature stays the same. Cold-blooded animals like lizards take on the temperature in their **environment**. If their environment is hot, they are hot. If it's cold, they are cold too.

The Sun heats planet Earth. Our planet and seven other planets circle the Sun in our **solar system**. An invisible pulling force called **gravity** from the Sun keeps the planets in their **orbits**.

The Sun is a star, not a planet. It is the closest star to Earth. That's why we can feel its heat and see its light.

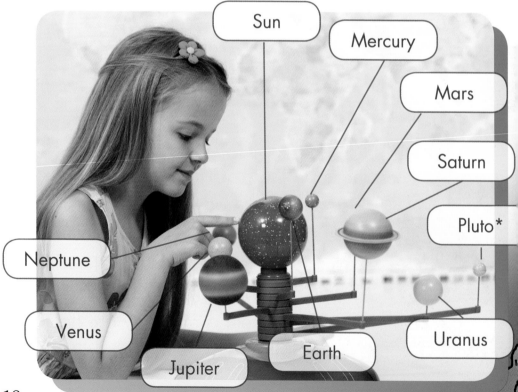

Sun

Mercury

Mars

Saturn

Pluto*

Neptune

Venus

Uranus

Earth

Jupiter

*Pluto is a dwarf planet on the rim of our Solar System.

Did You Know?

Space Cat:
All the planets have their own gravity. Earth's gravity keeps us from floating away.

Dog:
I'm happy with my paws on the ground!

Coral reefs are underwater ecosystems.

Sunlight is not a living thing, but all living things need sunlight to survive. In an **ecosystem**, animals and plants depend on each other and on sunlight, water, and soil. Plants send down roots into the soil. Sunlight and water make the plants grow. Some animals eat the plants. Other animals eat the plant eaters.

Each part of an ecosystem connects to all the other parts. Each part must be healthy

to keep the ecosystem in balance. If one part is hurt, the system won't work. If one part disappears, the whole ecosystem could disappear too.

Take care of Earth's ecosystems and all the systems that make up Y-O-U! How many systems did you find?

Try it!

Space Cat:
Float a green leaf in a clear glass of water. Leave it in a sunny place for an hour. The tiny bubbles you'll see are oxygen.

Glossary

Ancient From a time long, long ago

Communicate to give information

Energy the power to do work and activity

Environment the surroundings in which an animal or plant lives and grows

Gravity the force that pulls things toward the surface of a planet or star

Internet a giant network or system that connects computers all over the world

Mammals warm-blooded animals usually with hair or fur such as humans

Orbit one complete circle around a space object like a planet or moon

System a group of parts that work together to make something happen

Thermostat a device that controls temperature in a heating or cooling system

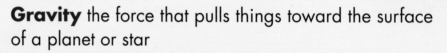

Learn More in the Library

Books

Ceceri, Kathy. *Robotics: Discover the Science and Technology of the Future.* Nomad Press, 2012.

Felix, Rebecca. *Electricity at Work.* Abdo Sandcastle, 2017.

Tieck, Sarah. *Circulatory System (Body Systems).* Abdo Buddy Books, 2011.

Web Sites

KidsHealth: How the body's systems work

http://kidshealth.org/en/kids/htbw/

STEM Works: Robotics & Coding Activities for Kids

http://stem-works.com/subjects/1-robotics/activities

index

air traffic control system, 8

carbon dioxide, 6

circulatory system, 7

communication systems, 10-11

ecosystem, 20-21

energy, 4

engineers, 3

gravity, 18

heating & cooling systems, 16-17

Internet, 10

plumbing systems, 14

respiratory system, 5

solar system, 18

transportation systems, 8-9